A Reading of Life, and Other Poems

George Meredith

Contents

Poem: A Reading of Life--The Vital Choice 7
Poem: A Reading of Life--With The Huntress 8
Poem: A Reading of Life--With The Persuader 10
Poem: A Reading of Life--The Test Of Manhood 21
Poem: The Cageing Of Ares 29
Poem: The Night-Walk 34
Poem: The Hueless Love 36
Poem: Song In The Songless 38
Poem: Union In Disseverance 38
Poem: The Burden Of Strength 39
Poem: The Main Regret 39
Poem: Alternation 40
Poem: Hawarden 41
Poem: At The Close 41
Poem: Forest History 42
Poem: A Garden Idyl 49
Poem: Foresight And Patience 52
Poem: The Invective of Achilles 62
Poem: The Invective of Achilles--V. 225 63
Poem: Marshalling Of The Achaians 64
Poem: Agamemnon In The Fight 65
Poem: Paris And Diomedes 66
Poem: Hypnos On Ida 67
Poem: Clash In Arms Of The Achaians And Trojans 67
Poem: The Horses Of Achilles 68
Poem: The Mares Of The Camargue 69

A READING OF LIFE, AND OTHER POEMS

BY
George Meredith

Poem: A Reading of Life--The Vital Choice

I.

Or shall we run with Artemis
Or yield the breast to Aphrodite?
Both are mighty;
Both give bliss;
Each can torture if divided;
Each claims worship undivided,
In her wake would have us wallow.

II.

Youth must offer on bent knees
Homage unto one or other;
Earth, the mother,
This decrees;
And unto the pallid Scyther
Either points us shun we either
Shun or too devoutly follow.

Poem: A Reading of Life--With The Huntress

Through the water-eye of night,
Midway between eve and dawn,
See the chase, the rout, the flight
In deep forest; oread, faun,
Goat-foot, antlers laid on neck;
Ravenous all the line for speed.
See yon wavy sparkle beck
Sign of the Virgin Lady's lead.
Down her course a serpent star
Coils and shatters at her heels;
Peals the horn exulting, peals
Plaintive, is it near or far.
Huntress, arrowy to pursue,
In and out of woody glen,
Under cliffs that tear the blue,
Over torrent, over fen,
She and forest, where she skims
Feathery, darken and relume:
Those are her white-lightning limbs
Cleaving loads of leafy gloom.
Mountains hear her and call back,
Shrewd with night: a frosty wail
Distant: her the emerald vale
Folds, and wonders in her track.
Now her retinue is lean,
Many rearward; streams the chase
Eager forth of covert; seen
One hot tide the rapturous race.

Quiver-charged and crescent-crowned,
Up on a flash the lighted mound
Leaps she, bow to shoulder, shaft
Strung to barb with archer's craft,
Legs like plaited lyre-chords, feet
Songs to see, past pitch of sweet.
Fearful swiftness they outrun,
Shaggy wildness, grey or dun,
Challenge, charge of tusks elude:
Theirs the dance to tame the rude;
Beast, and beast in manhood tame,
Follow we their silver flame.
Pride of flesh from bondage free,
Reaping vigour of its waste,
Marks her servitors, and she
Sanctifies the unembraced.
Nought of perilous she reeks;
Valour clothes her open breast;
Sweet beyond the thrill of sex;
Hallowed by the sex confessed.
Huntress arrowy to pursue,
Colder she than sunless dew,
She, that breath of upper air;
Ay, but never lyrist sang,
Draught of Bacchus never sprang
Blood the bliss of Gods to share,
High o'er sweep of eagle wings,
Like the run with her, when rings
Clear her rally, and her dart,
In the forest's cavern heart,
Tells of her victorious aim.
Then is pause and chatter, cheer,
Laughter at some satyr lame,

Looks upon the fallen deer,
Measuring his noble crest;
Here a favourite in her train,
Foremost mid her nymphs, caressed;
All applauded. Shall she reign
Worshipped? O to be with her there!
She, that breath of nimble air,
Lifts the breast to giant power.
Maid and man, and man and maid,
Who each other would devour
Elsewhere, by the chase betrayed,
There are comrades, led by her,
Maid-preserver, man-maker.

Poem: A Reading of Life--With The Persuader

Who murmurs, hither, hither: who
Where nought is audible so fills the ear?
Where nought is visible can make appear
A veil with eyes that waver through,
Like twilight's pledge of blessed night to come,
Or day most golden? All unseen and dumb,
She breathes, she moves, inviting flees,
Is lost, and leaves the thrilled desire
To clasp and strike a slackened lyre,
Till over smiles of hyacinth seas,
Flame in a crystal vessel sails
Beneath a dome of jewelled spray,
For land that drops the rosy day

On nights of throbbing nightingales.

Landward did the wonder flit,
Or heart's desire of her, all earth in it.
We saw the heavens fling down their rose;
On rapturous waves we saw her glide;
The pearly sea-shell half enclose;
The shoal of sea-nymphs flush the tide;
And we, afire to kiss her feet, no more
Behold than tracks along a startled shore,
With brightened edges of dark leaves that feign
An ambush hoped, as heartless night remain.

More closely, warmly: hither, hither! she,
The very she called forth by ripened blood
For its next breath of being, murmurs; she,
Allurement; she, fulfilment; she,
The stream within us urged to flood;
Man's cry, earth's answer, heaven's consent; O she,
Maid, woman and divinity;
Our over-earthly, inner-earthly mate
Unmated; she, our hunger and our fruit
Untasted; she our written fate
Unread; Life's flowering, Life's root:
Unread, divined; unseen, beheld;
The evanescent, ever-present she,
Great Nature's stern necessity
In radiance clothed, to softness quelled;
With a sword's edge of sweetness keen to take
Our breath for bliss, our hearts for fulness break.

The murmur hushes down, the veil is rent.
Man's cry, earth's answer, heaven's consent,

Her form is given to pardoned sight,
And lets our mortal eyes receive
The sovereign loveliness of celestial white;
Adored by them who solitarily pace,
In dusk of the underworld's perpetual eve,
The paths among the meadow asphodel,
Remembering. Never there her face
Is planetary; reddens to shore sea-shell
Around such whiteness the enamoured air
Of noon that clothes her, never there.
Daughter of light, the joyful light,
She stands unveiled to nuptial sight,
Sweet in her disregard of aid
Divine to conquer or persuade.
A fountain jets from moss; a flower
Bends gently where her sunset tresses shower.
By guerdon of her brilliance may be seen
With eyelids unabashed the passion's Queen.

Shorn of attendant Graces she can use
Her natural snares to make her will supreme.
A simple nymph it is, inclined to muse
Before the leader foot shall dip in stream:
One arm at curve along a rounded thigh;
Her firm new breasts each pointing its own way
A knee half bent to shade its fellow shy,
Where innocence, not nature, signals nay.
The bud of fresh virginity awaits
The wooer, and all roseate will she burst:
She touches on the hour of happy mates;
Still is she unaware she wakens thirst.

And while commanding blissful sight believe

It holds her as a body strained to breast,
Down on the underworld's perpetual eve
She plunges the possessor dispossessed;
And bids believe that image, heaving warm,
Is lost to float like torch-smoke after flame;
The phantom any breeze blows out of form;
A thirst's delusion, a defeated aim.

The rapture shed the torture weaves;
The direst blow on human heart she deals:
The pain to know the seen deceives;
Nought true but what insufferably feels.
And stabs of her delicious note,
That is as heavenly light to hearing, heard
Through shelter leaves, the laughter from her throat,
We answer as the midnight's morning's bird.

She laughs, she wakens gleeful cries;
In her delicious laughter part revealed;
Yet mother is she more of moans and sighs,
For longings unappeased and wounds unhealed.
Yet would she bless, it is her task to bless:
Yon folded couples, passing under shade,
Are her rich harvest; bidden caress, caress,
Consume the fruit in bloom; not disobeyed.
We dolorous complainers had a dream,
Wrought on the vacant air from inner fire,
We saw stand bare of her celestial beam
The glorious Goddess, and we dared desire.

Thereat are shown reproachful eyes, and lips
Of upward curl to meanings half obscure;
And glancing where a wood-nymph lightly skips

She nods: at once that creature wears her lure.
Blush of our being between birth and death:
Sob of our ripened blood for its next breath:
Her wily semblance nought of her denies;
Seems it the Goddess runs, the Goddess hies,
The generous Goddess yields. And she can arm
Her dwarfed and twisted with her secret charm;
Benevolent as Earth to feed her own.
Fully shall they be fed, if they beseech.
But scorn she has for them that walk alone;
Blanched men, starved women, whom no arts can pleach.
The men as chief of criminals she disdains,
And holds the reason in perceptive thought.
More pitiable, like rivers lacking rains,
Kissing cold stones, the women shrink for drought.
Those faceless discords, out of nature strayed,
Rank of the putrefaction ere decayed,
In impious singles bear the thorny wreaths:
Their lives are where harmonious Pleasure breathes
For couples crowned with flowers that burn in dew.
Comes there a tremor of night's forest horn
Across her garden from the insaner crew,
She darkens to malignity of scorn.
A shiver courses through her garden-grounds:
Grunt of the tusky boar, the baying hounds,
The hunter's shouts, are heard afar, and bring
Dead on her heart her crimsoned flower of Spring.
These, the irreverent of Life's design,
Division between natural and divine
Would cast; these vaunting barrenness for best,
In veins of gathered strength Life's tide arrest;
And these because the roses flood their cheeks,
Vow them in nature wise as when Love speaks.

With them is war; and well the Goddess knows
What undermines the race who mount the rose;
How the ripe moment, lodged in slumberous hours,
Enkindled by persuasion overpowers:
Why weak as are her frailer trailing weeds,
The strong when Beauty gleams o'er Nature's needs,
And timely guile unguarded finds them lie.
They who her sway withstand a sea defy,
At every point of juncture must be proof;
Nor look for mercy from the incessant surge
Her forces mixed of craft and passion urge
For the one whelming wave to spring aloof.
She, tenderness, is pitiless to them
Resisting in her godhead nature's truth.
No flower their face shall be, but writhen stem;
Their youth a frost, their age the dirge for youth.
These miserably disinclined,
The lamentably unembraced,
Insult the Pleasures Earth designed
To people and beflower the waste.
Wherefore the Pleasures pass them by:
For death they live, in life they die.

Her head the Goddess from them turns,
As from grey mounds of ashes in bronze urns.
She views her quivering couples unconsoled,
And of her beauty mirror they become,
Like orchard blossoms, apple, pear and plum,
Free of the cloud, beneath the flood of gold.
Crowned with wreaths that burn in dew,
Her couples whirl, sun-satiated,
Athirst for shade, they sigh, they wed,
They play the music made of two:

Oldest of earth, earth's youngest till earth's end:
Cunninger than the numbered strings,
For melodies, for harmonies,
For mastered discords, and the things
Not vocable, whose mysteries
Are inmost Love's, Life's reach of Life extend.

Is it an anguish overflowing shame
And the tongue's pudency confides to her,
With eyes of embers, breath of incense myrrh,
The woman's marrow in some dear youth's name,
Then is the Goddess tenderness
Maternal, and she has a sister's tones
Benign to soothe intemperate distress,
Divide despair from hope, and sighs from moans.
Her gentleness imparts exhaling ease
To those of her milk-bearer votaries
As warm of bosom-earth as she; of the source
Direct; erratic but in heart's excess;
Being mortal and ill-matched for Love's great force;
Like green leaves caught with flames by his impress.
And pray they under skies less overcast,
That swiftly may her star of eve descend,
Her lustrous morning star fly not too fast,
To lengthen blissful night will she befriend.

Unfailing her reply to woman's voice
In supplication instant. Is it man's,
She hears, approves his words, her garden scans,
And him: the flowers are various, he has choice.
Perchance his wound is deep; she listens long;
Enjoys what music fills the plaintive song;
And marks how he, who would be hawk at poise

Above the bird, his plaintive song enjoys.

She reads him when his humbled manhood weeps
To her invoked: distraction is implored.
A smile, and he is up on godlike leaps
Above, with his bright Goddess owned the adored.
His tales of her declare she condescends;
Can share his fires, not always goads and rends:
Moreover, quits a throne, and must enclose
A queenlier gem than woman's wayside rose.
She bends, he quickens; she breathes low, he springs
Enraptured; low she laughs, his woes disperse;
Aloud she laughs and sweeps his varied strings.
'Tis taught him how for touch of mournful verse
Rarely the music made of two ascends,
And Beauty's Queen some other way is won.
Or it may solve the riddle, that she lends
Herself to all, and yields herself to none,
Save heavenliest: though claims by men are raised
In hot assurance under shade of doubt:
And numerous are the images bepraised
As Beauty's Queen, should passion head the rout.

Be sure the ruddy hue is Love's: to woo
Love's Fountain we must mount the ruddy hue.
That is her garden's precept, seen where shines
Her blood-flower, and its unsought neighbour pines.
Daughter of light, the joyful light,
She bids her couples face full East,
Reflecting radiance, even when from her feast
Their outstretched arms brown deserts disunite,
The lion-haunted thickets hold apart.
In love the ruddy hue declares great heart;

High confidence in her whose aid is lent
To lovers lifting the tuned instrument,
Not one of rippled strings and funeral tone.
And doth the man pursue a tightened zone,
Then be it as the Laurel God he runs,
Confirmed to win, with countenance the Sun's.

Should pity bless the tremulous voice of woe
He lifts for pity, limp his offspring show.
For him requiring woman's arts to please
Infantile tastes with babe reluctances,
No race of giants! In the woman's veins
Persuasion ripely runs, through hers the pains.
Her choice of him, should kind occasion nod,
Aspiring blends the Titan with the God;
Yet unto dwarf and mortal, she, submiss
In her high Lady's mandate, yields the kiss;
And is it needed that Love's daintier brute
Be snared as hunter, she will tempt pursuit.
She is great Nature's ever intimate
In breast, and doth as ready handmaid wait,
Until perverted by her senseless male,
She plays the winding snake, the shrinking snail,
The flying deer, all tricks of evil fame,
Elusive to allure, since he grew tame.

Hence has the Goddess, Nature's earliest Power,
And greatest and most present, with her dower
Of the transcendent beauty, gained repute
For meditated guile. She laughs to hear
A charge her garden's labyrinths scarce confute,
Her garden's histories tell of to all near.
Let it be said, But less upon her guile

Doth she rely for her immortal smile.
Still let the rumour spread, and terror screens
To push her conquests by the simplest means.
While man abjures not lustihead, nor swerves
From earth's good labours, Beauty's Queen he serves.

Her spacious garden and her garden's grant
She offers in reward for handsome cheer:
Choice of the nymphs whose looks will slant
The secret down a dewy leer
Of corner eyelids into haze:
Many a fair Aphrosyne
Like flower-bell to honey-bee:
And here they flicker round the maze
Bewildering him in heart and head:
And here they wear the close demure,
With subtle peeps to reassure:
Others parade where love has bled,
And of its crimson weave their mesh:
Others to snap of fingers leap,
As bearing breast with love asleep.
These are her laughters in the flesh.
Or would she fit a warrior mood,
She lights her seeming unsubdued,
And indicates the fortress-key.
Or is it heart for heart that craves,
She flecks along a run of waves
The one to promise deeper sea.

Bands of her limpid primitives,
Or patterned in the curious braid,
Are the blest man's; and whatsoever he gives,
For what he gives is he repaid.

Good is it if by him 'tis held
He wins the fairest ever welled
From Nature's founts: she whispers it: Even I
Not fairer! and forbids him to deny,
Else little is he lover. Those he clasps,
Intent as tempest, worshipful as prayer, -
And be they doves or be they asps, -
Must seem to him the sovereignty fair;
Else counts he soon among life's wholly tamed.
Him whom from utter savage she reclaimed,
Half savage must he stay, would he be crowned
The lover. Else, past ripeness, deathward bound,
He reasons; and the totterer Earth detests,
Love shuns, grim logic screws in grasp, is he.
Doth man divide divine Necessity
From Joy, between the Queen of Beauty's breasts
A sword is driven; for those most glorious twain
Present her; armed to bless and to constrain.
Of this he perishes; not she, the throned
On rocks that spout their springs to the sacred mounts.
A loftier Reason out of deeper founts
Earth's chosen Goddess bears: by none disowned
While red blood runs to swell the pulse, she boasts,
And Beauty, like her star, descends the sky;
Earth's answer, heaven's consent unto man's cry,
Uplifted by the innumerable hosts.

Quickened of Nature's eye and ear,
When the wild sap at high tide smites
Within us; or benignly clear
To vision; or as the iris lights
On fluctuant waters; she is ours
Till set of man: the dreamed, the seen;

Flushing the world with odorous flowers:
A soft compulsion on terrene
By heavenly: and the world is hers
While hunger after Beauty spurs.

So is it sung in any space
She fills, with laugh at shallow laws
Forbidding love's devised embrace,
The music Beauty from it draws.

Poem: A Reading of Life--The Test Of Manhood

Like a flood river whirled at rocky banks,
An army issues out of wilderness,
With battle plucking round its ragged flanks;
Obstruction in the van; insane excess
Oft at the heart; yet hard the onward stress
Unto more spacious, where move ordered ranks,
And rise hushed temples built of shapely stone,
The work of hands not pledged to grind or slay.
They gave our earth a dress of flesh on bone;
A tongue to speak with answering heaven gave they.
Then was the gracious birth of man's new day;
Divided from the haunted night it shone.

That quiet dawn was Reverence; whereof sprang
Ethereal Beauty in full morningtide.
Another sun had risen to clasp his bride:
It was another earth unto him sang.

Came Reverence from the Huntress on her heights?
From the Persuader came it, in those vales
Whereunto she melodiously invites,
Her troops of eager servitors regales?
Not far those two great Powers of Nature speed
Disciple steps on earth when sole they lead;
Nor either points for us the way of flame.
From him predestined mightier it came;
His task to hold them both in breast, and yield
Their dues to each, and of their war be field.

The foes that in repulsion never ceased,
Must he, who once has been the goodly beast
Of one or other, at whose beck he ran,
Constrain to make him serviceable man;
Offending neither, nor the natural claim
Each pressed, denying, for his true man's name.

Ah, what a sweat of anguish in that strife
To hold them fast conjoined within him still;
Submissive to his will
Along the road of life!
And marvel not he wavered if at whiles
The forward step met frowns, the backward smiles.
For Pleasure witched him her sweet cup to drain;
Repentance offered ecstasy in pain.
Delicious licence called it Nature's cry;
Ascetic rigours crushed the fleshly sigh;
A tread on shingle timed his lame advance
Flung as the die of Bacchanalian Chance,
He of the troubled marching army leaned
On godhead visible, on godhead screened;

The radiant roseate, the curtained white;
Yet sharp his battle strained through day, through night.

He drank of fictions, till celestial aid
Might seem accorded when he fawned and prayed;
Sagely the generous Giver circumspect,
To choose for grants the egregious, his elect;
And ever that imagined succour slew
The soul of brotherhood whence Reverence drew.

In fellowship religion has its founts:
The solitary his own God reveres:
Ascend no sacred Mounts
Our hungers or our fears.
As only for the numbers Nature's care
Is shown, and she the personal nothing heeds,
So to Divinity the spring of prayer
From brotherhood the one way upward leads.
Like the sustaining air
Are both for flowers and weeds.
But he who claims in spirit to be flower,
Will find them both an air that doth devour.

Whereby he smelt his treason, who implored
External gifts bestowed but on the sword;
Beheld himself, with less and less disguise,
Through those blood-cataracts which dimmed his eyes,
His army's foe, condemned to strive and fail;
See a black adversary's ghost prevail;
Never, though triumphs hailed him, hope to win
While still the conflict tore his breast within.

Out of that agony, misread for those

Imprisoned Powers warring unappeased,
The ghost of his black adversary rose,
To smother light, shut heaven, show earth diseased.
And long with him was wrestling ere emerged
A mind to read in him the reflex shade
Of its fierce torment; this way, that way urged;
By craven compromises hourly swayed.

Crouched as a nestling, still its wings untried,
The man's mind opened under weight of cloud.
To penetrate the dark was it endowed;
Stood day before a vision shooting wide.
Whereat the spectral enemy lost form;
The traversed wilderness exposed its track.
He felt the far advance in looking back;
Thence trust in his foot forward through the storm.

Under the low-browed tempest's eye of ire,
That ere it lightened smote a coward heart,
Earth nerved her chastened son to hail athwart
All ventures perilous his shrouded Sire;
A stranger still, religiously divined;
Not yet with understanding read aright.
But when the mind, the cherishable mind,
The multitude's grave shepherd, took full flight,
Himself as mirror raised among his kind,
He saw, and first of brotherhood had sight:
Knew that his force to fly, his will to see,
His heart enlarged beyond its ribbed domain,
Had come of many a grip in mastery,
Which held conjoined the hostile rival twain,
And of his bosom made him lord, to keep
The starry roof of his unruffled frame

Awake to earth, to heaven, and plumb the deep
Below, above, aye with a wistful aim.

The mastering mind in him, by tempests blown,
By traitor inmates baited, upward burned;
Perforce of growth, the Master mind discerned,
The Great Unseen, nowise the Dark Unknown.
To whom unwittingly did he aspire
In wilderness, where bitter was his need:
To whom in blindness, as an earthy seed
For light and air, he struck through crimson mire.
But not ere he upheld a forehead lamp,
And viewed an army, once the seeming doomed,
All choral in its fruitful garden camp,
The spiritual the palpable illumed.

This gift of penetration and embrace,
His prize from tidal battles lost or won,
Reveals the scheme to animate his race:
How that it is a warfare but begun;
Unending; with no Power to interpose;
No prayer, save for strength to keep his ground,
Heard of the Highest; never battle's close,
The victory complete and victor crowned:
Nor solace in defeat, save from that sense
Of strength well spent, which is the strength renewed.
In manhood must he find his competence;
In his clear mind the spiritual food:
God being there while he his fight maintains;
Throughout his mind the Master Mind being there,
While he rejects the suicide despair;
Accepts the spur of explicable pains;
Obedient to Nature, not her slave:

Her lord, if to her rigid laws he bows;
Her dust, if with his conscience he plays knave,
And bids the Passions on the Pleasures browse:-
Whence Evil in a world unread before;
That mystery to simple springs resolved.
His God the Known, diviner to adore,
Shows Nature's savage riddles kindly solved.
Inconscient, insensitive, she reigns
In iron laws, though rapturous fair her face.
Back to the primal brute shall he retrace
His path, doth he permit to force her chains
A soft Persuader coursing through his veins,
An icy Huntress stringing to the chase:
What one the flash disdains;
What one so gives it grace.

But is he rightly manful in her eyes,
A splendid bloodless knight to gain the skies,
A blood-hot son of Earth by all her signs,
Desireing and desireable he shines;
As peaches, that have caught the sun's uprise
And kissed warm gold till noonday, even as vines.
Earth fills him with her juices, without fear
That she will cast him drunken down the steeps.
All woman is she to this man most dear;
He sows for bread, and she in spirit reaps:
She conscient, she sensitive, in him;
With him enwound, his brave ambition hers:
By him humaner made; by his keen spurs
Pricked to race past the pride in giant limb,
Her crazy adoration of big thews,
Proud in her primal sons, when crags they hurled,
Were thunder spitting lightnings on the world

In daily deeds, and she their evening Muse.

This man, this hero, works not to destroy;
This godlike--as the rock in ocean stands; -
He of the myriad eyes, the myriad hands
Creative; in his edifice has joy.
How strength may serve for purity is shown
When he himself can scourge to make it clean.
Withal his pitch of pride would not disown
A sober world that walks the balanced mean
Between its tempters, rarely overthrown:
And such at times his army's march has been.

Near is he to great Nature in the thought
Each changing Season intimately saith,
That nought save apparition knows the death;
To the God-lighted mind of man 'tis nought.
She counts not loss a word of any weight;
It may befal his passions and his greeds
To lose their treasures, like the vein that bleeds,
But life gone breathless will she reinstate.

Close on the heart of Earth his bosom beats,
When he the mandate lodged in it obeys,
Alive to breast a future wrapped in haze,
Strike camp, and onward, like the wind's cloud-fleets.
Unresting she, unresting he, from change
To change, as rain of cloud, as fruit of rain;
She feels her blood-tree throbbing in her grain,
Yet skyward branched, with loftier mark and range.

No miracle the sprout of wheat from clod,
She knows, nor growth of man in grisly brute;

But he, the flower at head and soil at root,
Is miracle, guides he the brute to God.
And that way seems he bound; that way the road,
With his dark-lantern mind, unled, alone,
Wearifully through forest-tracts unsown,
He travels, urged by some internal goad.

Dares he behold the thing he is, what thing
He would become is in his mind its child;
Astir, demanding birth to light and wing;
For battle prompt, by pleasure unbeguiled.
So moves he forth in faith, if he has made
His mind God's temple, dedicate to truth.
Earth's nourishing delights, no more gainsaid,
He tastes, as doth the bridegroom rich in youth.
Then knows he Love, that beckons and controls;
The star of sky upon his footway cast;
Then match in him who holds his tempters fast,
The body's love and mind's, whereof the soul's.
Then Earth her man for woman finds at last,
To speed the pair unto her goal of goals.

Or is't the widowed's dream of her new mate?
Seen has she virulent days of heat in flood;
The sly Persuader snaky in his blood;
With her the barren Huntress alternate;
His rough refractory off on kicking heels
To rear; the man dragged rearward, shamed, amazed;
And as a torrent stream where cattle grazed,
His tumbled world. What, then, the faith she feels?
May not his aspect, like her own so fair
Reflexively, the central force belie,
And he, the once wild ocean storming sky,

Be rebel at the core? What hope is there?

'Tis that in each recovery he preserves,
Between his upper and his nether wit,
Sense of his march ahead, more brightly lit;
He less the shaken thing of lusts and nerves;
With such a grasp upon his brute as tells
Of wisdom from that vile relapsing spun.
A Sun goes down in wasted fire, a Sun
Resplendent springs, to faith refreshed compels.

Poem: The Cageing Of Ares

[Iliad, v. V. 385--Dedicated to the Council at The Hague.]

How big of breast our Mother Gaea laughed
At sight of her boy Giants on the leap
Each over other as they neighboured home,
Fronting the day's descent across green slopes,
And up fired mountain crags their shadows danced.
Close with them in their fun, she scarce could guess,
Though these two billowy urchins reeked of craft,
It signalled some adventurous master-trick
To set Olympians buzzing in debate,
Lest it might be their godhead undermined,
The Tyranny menaced. Ephialtes high
On shoulders of his brother Otos waved
For the bull-bellowings given to grand good news,
Compact, complexioned in his gleeful roar

While Otos aped the prisoner's wrists and knees,
With doleful sniffs between recurrent howls;
Till Gaea's lap receiving them, they stretched,
And both upon her bosom shaken to speech,
Burst the hot story out of throats of both,
Like rocky head-founts, baffling in their glut
The hurried spout. And as when drifting storm
Disburdened loses clasp of here and yon
A peak, a forest mound, a valley's gleam
Of grass and the river's crooks and snaky coils,
Signification marvellous she caught,
Through gurglings of triumphant jollity,
Which now engulphed and now gave eye; at last
Subsided, and the serious naked deed,
With mountain-cloud of laughter banked around,
Stood in her sight confirmed: she could believe
That these, her sprouts of promise, her most prized,
These two made up of lion, bear and fox,
Her sportive, suckling mammoths, her young joy,
Still by the reckoning infants among men,
Had done the deed to strike the Titan host
In envy dumb, in envious heart elate:
These two combining strength and craft had snared,
Enmeshed, bound fast with thongs, discreetly caged
The blood-shedder, the terrible Lord of War;
Destroyer, ravager, superb in plumes;
The barren furrower of anointed fields;
The scarlet heel in towns, foul smoke to sky,
Her hated enemy, too long her scourge:
Great Ares. And they gagged his trumpet mouth
When they had seized on his implacable spear,
Hugged him to reedy helplessness despite
His godlike fury startled from amaze.

For he had eyed them nearing him in play,
The giant cubs, who gambolled and who snarled,
Unheeding his fell presence, by the mount
Ossa, beside a brushwood cavern; there
On Earth's original fisticuffs they called
For ease of sharp dispute: whereat the God,
Approving, deemed that sometime trained to arms,
Good servitors of Ares they would be,
And ply the pointed spear to dominate
Their rebel restless fellows, villain brood
Vowed to defy Immortals. So it chanced
Amusedly he watched them, and as one
The lusty twain were on him and they had him.
Breath to us, Powers of air, for laughter loud!
Cock of Olympus he, superb in plumes!
Bound like a wheaten sheaf by those two babes!
Because they knew our Mother Gaea loathed him,
Knew him the famine, pestilence and waste;
A desolating fire to blind the sight
With splendour built of fruitful things in ashes;
The gory chariot-wheel on cries for justice;
Her deepest planted and her liveliest voice,
Heard from the babe as from the broken crone.
Behold him in his vessel of bronze encased,
And tumbled down the cave. But rather look -
Ah, that the woman tattler had not sought,
Of all the Gods to let her secret fly,
Hermes, after the thirteen songful months!
Prompting the Dexterous to work his arts,
And shatter earth's delirious holiday,
Then first, as where the fountain runs a stream,
Resolving to composure on its throbs.
But see her in the Seasons through that year;

That one glad year and the fair opening month.
Had never our Great Mother such sweet face!
War with her, gentle war with her, each day
Her sons and daughters urged; at eve were flung,
On the morrow stood to challenge; in their strength
Renewed, indomitable; whereof they won,
From hourly wrestlings up to shut of lids,
Her ready secret: the abounding life
Returned for valiant labour: she and they
Defeated and victorious turn by turn;
By loss enriched, by overthrow restored.
Exchange of powers of this conflict came;
Defacement none, nor ever squandered force.
Is battle nature's mandate, here it reigned,
As music unto the hand that smote the strings;
And she the rosier from their showery brows,
They fruitful from her ploughed and harrowed breast.
Back to the primal rational of those
Who suck the teats of milky earth, and clasp
Stability in hatred of the insane,
Man stepped; with wits less fearful to pronounce
The mortal mind's concept of earth's divorced
Above; those beautiful, those masterful,
Those lawless. High they sit, and if descend,
Descend to reap, not sowing. Is it just?
Earth in her happy children asked that word,
Whereto within their breast was her reply.
Those beautiful, those masterful, those lawless,
Enjoy the life prolonged, outleap the years;
Yet they ('twas the Great Mother's voice inspired
The audacious thought), they, glorious over dust,
Outleap not her; disrooted from her soar,
To meet the certain fate of earth's divorced,

And clap lame wings across a wintry haze,
Up to the farthest bourne: immortal still,
Thenceforth innocuous; lovelier than when ruled
The Tyranny. This her voice within them told,
When softly the Great Mother chid her sons
Not of the giant brood, who did create
Those lawless Gods, first offspring of our brain
Set moving by an abject blood, that waked
To wanton under elements more benign,
And planted aliens on Olympian heights; -
Imagination's cradle poesy
Become a monstrous pressure upon men; -
Foes of good Gaea; until dispossessed
By light from her, born of the love of her,
Their lordship the illumined brain rejects
For earth's beneficent, the sons of Law,
Her other name. So spake she in their heart,
Among the wheat-blades proud of stalk; beneath
Young vine-leaves pushing timid fingers forth,
Confidently to cling. And when brown corn
Swayed armied ranks with softened cricket song,
With gold necks bent for any zephyr's kiss;
When vine-roots daily down a rubble soil
Drank fire of heaven athirst to swell the grape;
When swelled the grape, and in it held a ray,
Rich issue of the embrace of heaven and earth;
The very eye of passion drowsed by excess,
And yet a burning lion for the spring;
Then in that time of general cherishment,
Sweet breathing balm and flutes by cool wood-side,
He the harsh rouser of ire being absent, caged,
Then did good Gaea's children gratefully
Lift hymns to Gods they judged, but praised for peace,

Delightful Peace, that answers Reason's call
Harmoniously and images her Law;
Reflects, and though short-lived as then, revives,
In memories made present on the brain
By natural yearnings, all the happy scenes;
The picture of an earth allied to heaven;
Between them the known smile behind black masks;
Rightly their various moods interpreted;
And frolic because toilful children borne
With larger comprehension of Earth's aim
At loftier, clearer, sweeter, by their aid.

Poem: The Night-Walk

Awakes for me and leaps from shroud
All radiantly the moon's own night
Of folded showers in streamer cloud;
Our shadows down the highway white
Or deep in woodland woven-boughed,
With yon and yon a stem alight.

I see marauder runagates
Across us shoot their dusky wink;
I hear the parliament of chats
In haws beside the river's brink;
And drops the vole off alder-banks,
To push his arrow through the stream.
These busy people had our thanks
For tickling sight and sound, but theme

They were not more than breath we drew
Delighted with our world's embrace:
The moss-root smell where beeches grew,
And watered grass in breezy space;
The silken heights, of ghostly bloom
Among their folds, by distance draped.
'Twas Youth, rapacious to consume,
That cried to have its chaos shaped:
Absorbing, little noting, still
Enriched, and thinking it bestowed;
With wistful looks on each far hill
For something hidden, something owed.
Unto his mantled sister, Day
Had given the secret things we sought
And she was grave and saintly gay;
At times she fluttered, spoke her thought;
She flew on it, then folded wings,
In meditation passing lone,
To breathe around the secret things,
Which have no word, and yet are known;
Of thirst for them are known, as air
Is health in blood: we gained enough
By this to feel it honest fare;
Impalpable, not barren, stuff.

A pride of legs in motion kept
Our spirits to their task meanwhile,
And what was deepest dreaming slept:
The posts that named the swallowed mile;
Beside the straight canal the hut
Abandoned; near the river's source
Its infant chirp; the shortest cut;
The roadway missed; were our discourse;

At times dear poets, whom some view
Transcendent or subdued evoked
To speak the memorable, the true,
The luminous as a moon uncloaked;
For proof that there, among earth's dumb,
A soul had passed and said our best.
Or it might be we chimed on some
Historic favourite's astral crest,
With part to reverence in its gleam,
And part to rivalry the shout:
So royal, unuttered, is youth's dream
Of power within to strike without.
But most the silences were sweet,
Like mothers' breasts, to bid it feel
It lived in such divine conceit
As envies aught we stamp for real.

To either then an untold tale
Was Life, and author, hero, we.
The chapters holding peaks to scale,
Or depths to fathom, made our glee;
For we were armed of inner fires,
Unbled in us the ripe desires;
And passion rolled a quiet sea,
Whereon was Love the phantom sail.

Poem: The Hueless Love

Unto that love must we through fire attain,

Which those two held as breath of common air;
The hands of whom were given in bond elsewhere;
Whom Honour was untroubled to restrain.

Midway the road of our life's term they met,
And one another knew without surprise;
Nor cared that beauty stood in mutual eyes;
Nor at their tardy meeting nursed regret.

To them it was revealed how they had found
The kindred nature and the needed mind;
The mate by long conspiracy designed;
The flower to plant in sanctuary ground.

Avowed in vigilant solicitude
For either, what most lived within each breast
They let be seen: yet every human test
Demanding righteousness approved them good.

She leaned on a strong arm, and little feared
Abandonment to help if heaved or sank
Her heart at intervals while Love looked blank,
Life rosier were she but less revered.

An arm that never shook did not obscure
Her woman's intuition of the bliss -
Their tempter's moment o'er the black abyss,
Across the narrow plank--he could abjure.

Then came a day that clipped for him the thread,
And their first touch of lips, as he lay cold,
Was all of earthly in their love untold,
Beyond all earthly known to them who wed.

So has there come the gust at South-west flung
By sudden volt on eves of freezing mist,
When sister snowflake sister snowdrop kissed,
And one passed out, and one the bell-head hung.

Poem: Song In The Songless

They have no song, the sedges dry,
And still they sing.
It is within my breast they sing,
As I pass by.
Within my breast they touch a string,
They wake a sigh.
There is but sound of sedges dry;
In me they sing.

Poem: Union In Disseverance

Sunset worn to its last vermilion he;
She that star overhead in slow descent:
That white star with the front of angel she;
He undone in his rays of glory spent

Halo, fair as the bow-shot at his rise,
He casts round her, and knows his hour of rest
Incomplete, were the light for which he dies,
Less like joy of the dove that wings to nest.

Lustrous momently, near on earth she sinks;
Life's full throb over breathless and abased:
Yet stand they, though impalpable the links,
One, more one than the bridally embraced.

Poem: The Burden Of Strength

If that thou hast the gift of strength, then know
Thy part is to uplift the trodden low;
Else in a giant's grasp until the end
A hopeless wrestler shall thy soul contend.

Poem: The Main Regret

[Written for the Charing Cross Album]

I.

Seen, too clear and historic within us, our sins of omission

Frown when the Autumn days strike us all ruthlessly bare.
They of our mortal diseases find never healing physician;
Errors they of the soul, past the one hope to repair.

II.

Sunshine might we have been unto seed under soil, or have scattered
Seed to ascendant suns brighter than any that shone.
Even the limp-legged beggar a sick desperado has flattered
Back to a half-sloughed life cheered by the mere human tone.

Poem: Alternation

Between the fountain and the rill
I passed, and saw the mighty will
To leap at sky; the careless run,
As earth would lead her little son.

Beneath them throbs an urgent well,
That here is play, and there is war.
I know not which had most to tell
Of whence we spring and what we are.

Poem: Hawarden

When comes the lighted day for men to read
Life's meaning, with the work before their hands
Till this good gift of breath from debt is freed,
Earth will not hear her children's wailful bands
Deplore the chieftain fall'n in sob and dirge;
Nor they look where is darkness, but on high.
The sun that dropped down our horizon's verge,
Illumes his labours through the travelled sky,
Now seen in sum, most glorious; and 'tis known
By what our warrior wrought we hold him fast.
A splendid image built of man has flown;
His deeds inspired of God outstep a Past.
Ours the great privilege to have had one
Among us who celestial tasks has done.

Poem: At The Close

To Thee, dear God of Mercy, both appeal,
Who straightway sound the call to arms. Thou know'st;
And that black spot in each embattled host,
Spring of the blood-stream, later wilt reveal.
Now is it red artillery and white steel;
Till on a day will ring the victor's boast,

That 'tis Thy chosen towers uppermost,
Where Thy rejected grovels under heel.
So in all times of man's descent insane
To brute, did strength and craft combining strike,
Even as a God of Armies, his fell blow.
But at the close he entered Thy domain,
Dear God of Mercy, and if lion-like
He tore the fall'n, the Eternal was his Foe.

Poem: Forest History

I.

Beneath the vans of doom did men pass in.
Heroic who came out; for round them hung
A wavering phantom's red volcano tongue,
With league-long lizard tail and fishy fin:

II.

Old Earth's original Dragon; there retired
To his last fastness; overthrown by few.
Him a laborious thrust of roadway slew.
Then man to play devorant straight was fired.

III.

More intimate became the forest fear
While pillared darkness hatched malicious life

At either elbow, wolf or gnome or knife
And wary slid the glance from ear to ear.

IV.

In chillness, like a clouded lantern-ray,
The forest's heart of fog on mossed morass,
On purple pool and silky cotton-grass,
Revealed where lured the swallower byway.

V.

Dead outlook, flattened back with hard rebound
Off walls of distance, left each mounted height.
It seemed a giant hag-fiend, churning spite
Of humble human being, held the ground.

VI.

Through friendless wastes, through treacherous woodland, slow
The feet sustained by track of feet pursued
Pained steps, and found the common brotherhood
By sign of Heaven indifferent, Nature foe.

VII.

Anon a mason's work amazed the sight,
And long-frocked men, called Brothers, there abode.
They pointed up, bowed head, and dug and sowed;
Whereof was shelter, loaf, and warm firelight.

VIII.

What words they taught were nails to scratch the head.
Benignant works explained the chanting brood.
Their monastery lit black solitude,
As one might think a star that heavenward led.

IX.

Uprose a fairer nest for weary feet,
Like some gold flower nightly inward curled,
Where gentle maidens fled a roaring world,
Or played with it, and had their white retreat.

X.

Into big books of metal clasps they pored.
They governed, even as men; they welcomed lays.
The treasures women are whose aim is praise,
Was shown in them: the Garden half restored.

XI.

A deluge billow scoured the land off seas,
With widened jaws, and slaughter was its foam.
For food, for clothing, ambush, refuge, home,
The lesser savage offered bogs and trees.

XII.

Whence reverence round grey-haired story grew:
And inmost spots of ancient horror shone

As temples under beams of trials bygone;
For in them sang brave times with God in view.

XIII.

Till now trim homesteads bordered spaces green,
Like night's first little stars through clearing showers.
Was rumoured how a castle's falcon towers
The wilderness commanded with fierce mien.

XIV.

Therein a serious Baron stuck his lance;
For minstrel songs a beauteous Dame would pout.
Gay knights and sombre, felon or devout,
Pricked onward, bound for their unsung romance.

XV.

It might be that two errant lords across
The block of each came edged, and at sharp cry
They charged forthwith, the better man to try.
One rode his way, one couched on quiet moss.

XVI.

Perchance a lady sweet, whose lord lay slain,
The robbers into gruesome durance drew.
Swift should her hero come, like lightning's blue!
She prayed for him, as crackling drought for rain.

XVII.

As we, that ere the worst her hero haps,
Of Angels guided, nigh that loathly den:
A toady cave beside an ague fen,
Where long forlorn the lone dog whines and yaps.

XVIII.

By daylight now the forest fear could read
Itself, and at new wonders chuckling went.
Straight for the roebuck's neck the bowman spent
A dart that laughed at distance and at speed.

XIX.

Right loud the bugle's hallali elate
Rang forth of merry dingles round the tors;
And deftest hand was he from foreign wars,
But soon he hailed the home-bred yeoman mate.

XX.

Before the blackbird pecked the turf they woke;
At dawn the deer's wet nostrils blew their last.
To forest, haunt of runs and prime repast,
With paying blows, the yokel strained his yoke.

XXI.

The city urchin mooned on forest air,
On grassy sweeps and flying arrows, thick

As swallows o'er smooth streams, and sighed him sick
For thinking that his dearer home was there.

XXII.

Familiar, still unseized, the forest sprang
An old-world echo, like no mortal thing.
The hunter's horn might wind a jocund ring,
But held in ear it had a chilly clang.

XXIII.

Some shadow lurked aloof of ancient time;
Some warning haunted any sound prolonged,
As though the leagues of woodland held them wronged
To hear an axe and see a township climb.

XXIV.

The forest's erewhile emperor at eve
Had voice when lowered heavens drummed for gales.
At midnight a small people danced the dales,
So thin that they might dwindle through a sieve

XXV.

Ringed mushrooms told of them, and in their throats,
Old wives that gathered herbs and knew too much.
The pensioned forester beside his crutch,
Struck showers from embers at those bodeful notes.

XXVI.

Came then the one, all ear, all eye, all heart;
Devourer, and insensibly devoured;
In whom the city over forest flowered,
The forest wreathed the city's drama-mart.

XXVII.

There found he in new form that Dragon old,
From tangled solitudes expelled; and taught
How blindly each its antidote besought;
For either's breath the needs of either told.

XXVIII.

Now deep in woods, with song no sermon's drone,
He showed what charm the human concourse works:
Amid the press of men, what virtue lurks
Where bubble sacred wells of wildness lone.

XXIX.

Our conquest these: if haply we retain
The reverence that ne'er will overrun
Due boundaries of realms from Nature won,
Nor let the poet's awe in rapture wane.

Poem: A Garden Idyl

With sagest craft Arachne worked
Her web, and at a corner lurked,
Awaiting what should plump her soon,
To case it in the death-cocoon.
Sagaciously her home she chose
For visits that would never close;
Inside my chalet-porch her feast
Plucked all the winds but chill North-east.

The finished structure, bar on bar,
Had snatched from light to form a star,
And struck on sight, when quick with dews,
Like music of the very Muse.
Great artists pass our single sense;
We hear in seeing, strung to tense;
Then haply marvel, groan mayhap,
To think such beauty means a trap.
But Nature's genius, even man's
At best, is practical in plans;
Subservient to the needy thought,
However rare the weapon wrought.
As long as Nature holds it good
To urge her creatures' quest for food
Will beauty stamp the just intent
Of weapons upon service bent.
For beauty is a flower of roots
Embedded lower than our boots;
Out of the primal strata springs,

And shows for crown of useful things

Arachne's dream of prey to size
Aspired; so she could nigh despise
The puny specks the breezes round
Supplied, and let them shake unwound;
Assured of her fat fly to come;
Perhaps a blue, the spider's plum;
Who takes the fatal odds in fight,
And gives repast an appetite,
By plunging, whizzing, till his wings
Are webbed, and in the lists he swings,
A shrouded lump, for her to see
Her banquet in her victory.

This matron of the unnumbered threads,
One day of dandelions' heads
Distributing their gray perruques
Up every gust, I watched with looks
Discreet beside the chalet-door;
And gracefully a light wind bore,
Direct upon my webster's wall,
A monster in the form of ball;
The mildest captive ever snared,
That neither struggled nor despaired,
On half the net invading hung,
And plain as in her mother tongue,
While low the weaver cursed her lures,
Remarked, "You have me; I am yours."

Thrice magnified, in phantom shape,
Her dream of size she saw, agape.
Midway the vast round-raying beard

A desiccated midge appeared;
Whose body pricked the name of meal,
Whose hair had growth in earth's unreal;
Provocative of dread and wrath,
Contempt and horror, in one froth,
Inextricable, insensible,
His poison presence there would dwell,
Declaring him her dream fulfilled,
A catch to compliment the skilled;
And she reduced to beaky skin,
Disgraceful among kith and kin

Against her corner, humped and aged,
Arachne wrinkled, past enraged,
Beyond disgust or hope in guile.
Ridiculously volatile
He seemed to her last spark of mind;
And that in pallid ash declined
Beneath the blow by knowledge dealt,
Wherein throughout her frame she felt
That he, the light wind's libertine,
Without a scoff, without a grin,
And mannered like the courtly few,
Who merely danced when light winds blew,
Impervious to beak and claws,
Tradition's ruinous Whitebeard was;
Of whom, as actors in old scenes,
Had grannam weavers warned their weans,
With word, that less than feather-weight,
He smote the web like bolt of Fate.

This muted drama, hour by hour,
I watched amid a world in flower,

Ere yet Autumnal threads had laid
Their gray-blue o'er the grass's blade,
And still along the garden-run
The blindworm stretched him, drunk of sun.
Arachne crouched unmoved; perchance
Her visitor performed a dance;
She puckered thinner; he the same
As when on that light wind he came.

Next day was told what deeds of night
Were done; the web had vanished quite;
With it the strange opposing pair;
And listless waved on vacant air,
For her adieu to heart's content,
A solitary filament.

Poem: Foresight And Patience

Sprung of the father blood, the mother brain,
Are they who point our pathway and sustain.
They rarely meet; one soars, one walks retired.
When they do meet, it is our earth inspired.

To see Life's formless offspring and subdue
Desire of times unripe, we have these two,
Whose union is right reason: join they hands,
The world shall know itself and where it stands;
What cowering angel and what upright beast
Make man, behold, nor count the low the least,

Nor less the stars have round it than its flowers.
When these two meet, a point of time is ours.

As in a land of waterfalls, that flow
Smooth for the leap on their great voice below,
Some eddies near the brink borne swift along,
Will capture hearing with the liquid song,
So, while the headlong world's imperious force
Resounded under, heard I these discourse.

First words, where down my woodland walk she led,
To her blind sister Patience, Foresight said:

- Your faith in me appals, to shake my own,
When still I find you in this mire alone.

- The few steps taken at a funeral pace
By men had slain me but for those you trace.

- Look I once back, a broken pinion I:
Black as the rebel angels rained from sky!

- Needs must you drink of me while here you live,
And make me rich in feeling I can give.

- A brave To-be is dawn upon my brow:
Yet must I read my sister for the How.
My daisy better knows her God of beams
Than doth an eagle that to mount him seems.
She hath the secret never fieriest reach
Of wing shall master till men hear her teach.

- Liker the clod flaked by the driving plough,

My semblance when I have you not as now.
The quiet creatures who escape mishap
Bear likeness to pure growths of the green sap:
A picture of the settled peace desired
By cowards shunning strife or strivers tired.
I listen at their breasts: is there no jar
Of wrestlings and of stranglings, dead they are,
And such a picture as the piercing mind
Ranks beneath vegetation. Not resigned
Are my true pupils while the world is brute.
What edict of the stronger keeps me mute,
Stronger impels the motion of my heart.
I am not Resignation's counterpart.
If that I teach, 'tis little the dry word,
Content, but how to savour hope deferred.
We come of earth, and rich of earth may be;
Soon carrion if very earth are we!
The coursing veins, the constant breath, the use
Of sleep, declare that strife allows short truce;
Unless we clasp decay, accept defeat,
And pass despised; "a-cold for lack of heat,"
Like other corpses, but without death's plea.

- My sister calls for battle; is it she?

- Rather a world of pressing men in arms,
Than stagnant, where the sensual piper charms
Each drowsy malady and coiling vice
With dreams of ease whereof the soul pays price!
No home is here for peace while evil breeds,
While error governs, none; and must the seeds
You sow, you that for long have reaped disdain,
Lie barren at the doorway of the brain,

Let stout contention drive deep furrows, blood
Moisten, and make new channels of its flood!

- My sober little maid, when we meet first,
Drinks of me ever with an eager thirst.
So can I not of her till circumstance
Drugs cravings. Here we see how men advance
A doubtful foot, but circle if much stirred,
Like dead weeds on whipped waters. Shout the word
Prompting their hungers, and they grandly march,
As to band-music under Victory's arch.
Thus was it, and thus is it; save that then
The beauty of frank animals had men.

- Observe them, and down rearward for a term,
Gaze to the primal twistings of the worm.
Thence look this way, across the fields that show
Men's early form of speech for Yes and No.
My sister a bruised infant's utterance had;
And issuing stronger, to mankind 'twas mad.
I knew my home where I had choice to feel
The toad beneath a harrow or a heel.

- Speak of this Age.

- When you it shall discern
Bright as you are, to me the Age will turn.

- For neither of us has it any care;
Its learning is through Science to despair.

- Despair lies down and grovels, grapples not
With evil, casts the burden of its lot.

This Age climbs earth.

- To challenge heaven.

- Not less
The lower deeps. It laughs at Happiness!
That know I, though the echoes of it wail,
For one step upward on the crags you scale.
Brave is the Age wherein the word will rust,
Which means our soul asleep or body's lust,
Until from warmth of many breasts, that beat
A temperate common music, sunlike heat
The happiness not predatory sheds!

- But your fierce Yes and No of butting heads,
Now rages to outdo a horny Past.
Shades of a wild Destroyer on the vast
Are thrown by every novel light upraised.
The world's whole round smokes ominously, amazed
And trembling as its pregnant AEtna swells.
Combustibles on hot combustibles
Run piling, for one spark to roll in fire
The mountain-torrent of infernal ire
And leave the track of devils where men built.
Perceptive of a doom, the sinner's guilt
Confesses in a cry for help shrill loud,
If drops the chillness of a passing cloud,
To conscience, reason, human love; in vain:
None save they but the souls which them contain.
No extramural God, the God within
Alone gives aid to city charged with sin.
A world that for the spur of fool and knave,
Sweats in its laboratory, what shall save?

But men who ply their wits in such a school,
Must pray the mercy of the knave and fool.

- Much have I studied hard Necessity!
To know her Wisdom's mother, and that we
May deem the harshness of her later cries
In labour a sure goad to prick the wise,
If men among the warnings which convulse,
Can gravely dread without the craven's pulse.
Long ere the rising of this Age of ours,
The knave and fool were stamped as monstrous Powers.
Of human lusts and lassitudes they spring,
And are as lasting as the parent thing.
Yet numbering locust hosts, bent they to drill,
They might o'ermatch and have mankind at will.

Behold such army gathering: ours the spur,
No scattered foe to face, but Lucifer.
Not fool or knave is now the enemy
O'ershadowing men, 'tis Folly, Knavery!
A sea; nor stays that sea the bastioned beach.
Now must the brother soul alive in each,
His traitorous individual devildom
Hold subject lest the grand destruction come.
Dimly men see it menacing apace
To overthrow, perchance uproot the race.
Within, without, they are a field of tares:
Fruitfuller for them when the contest squares,
And wherefore warrior service they must yield,
Shines visible as life on either field.
That is my comfort, following shock on shock,
Which sets faith quaking on their firmest rock.
Since with his weapons, all the arms of Night,

Frail men have challenged Lucifer to fight,
Have matched in hostile ranks, enrolled, erect,
The human and Satanic intellect,
Determined for their uses to control
What forces on the earth and under roll,
Their granite rock runs igneous; now they stand
Pledged to the heavens for safety of their land.
They cannot learn save grossly, gross that are:
Through fear they learn whose aid is good in war.

- My sister, as I read them in my glass,
Their field of tares they take for pasture grass.
How waken them that have not any bent
Save browsing--the concrete indifferent!
Friend Lucifer supplies them solid stuff:
They fear not for the race when full the trough.
They have much fear of giving up the ghost;
And these are of mankind the unnumbered host.

- If I could see with you, and did not faint
In beating wing, the future I would paint.
Those massed indifferents will learn to quake:
Now meanwhile is another mass awake,
Once denser than the grunters of the sty.
If I could see with you! Could I but fly!

- The length of days that you with them have housed,
An outcast else, approves their cause espoused.

- O true, they have a cause, and woe for us,
While still they have a cause too piteous!
Yet, happy for us when, their cause defined,
They walk no longer with a stumbler blind,

And quicken in the virtue of their cause,
To think me a poor mouther of old saws!
I wait the issue of a battling Age;
The toilers with your "troughsters" now engage;
Instructing them through their acutest sense,
How close the dangers of indifference!
Already have my people shown their worth,
More love they light, which folds the love of Earth.
That love to love of labour leads: thence love
Of humankind--earth's incense flung above.

- Admit some other features: Faithless, mean;
Encased in matter; vowed to Gods obscene;
Contemptuous of the impalpable, it swells
On Doubt; for pastime swallows miracles;
And if I bid it face what _I_ observe,
Declares me hoodwinked by my optic nerve!

- Oft has your prophet, for reward of toil,
Seen nests of seeming cockatrices coil:
Disowned them as the unholiest of Time,
Which were his offspring, born of flame on slime.
Nor him, their sire, have known the filial fry:
As little as Time's earliest knew the sky.
Perchance among them shoots a lustrous flame
At intervals, in proof of whom they came.
To strengthen our foundations is the task
Of this tough Age; not in your beams to bask,
Though, lighted by your beams, down mining caves
The rock it blasts, the hoarded foulness braves.
My sister sees no round beyond her mood;
To hawk this Age has dressed her head in hood.
Out of the course of ancient ruts and grooves,

It moves: O much for me to say it moves!
About his AEthiop Highlands Nile is Nile,
Though not the stream of the paternal smile:
And where his tide of nourishment he drives,
An Abyssinian wantonness revives.
Calm as his lotus-leaf to-day he swims;
He is the yellow crops, the rounded limbs,
The Past yet flowing, the fair time that fills;
Breath of all mouths and grist of many mills.

To-morrow, warning none with tempest-showers,
He is the vast Insensate who devours
His golden promise over leagues of seed,
Then sits in a smooth lake upon the deed.
The races which on barbarous force begin,
Inherit onward of their origin,
And cancelled blessings will the current length
Reveal till they know need of shaping strength.
'Tis not in men to recognize the need
Before they clash in hosts, in hosts they bleed.
Then may sharp suffering their nature grind;
Of rabble passions grow the chieftain Mind.
Yet mark where still broad Nile boasts thousands fed,
For tens up the safe mountains at his head.
Few would be fed, not far his course prolong,
Save for the troublous blood which makes him strong.

- That rings of truth! More do your people thrive;
Your Many are more merrily alive
Than erewhile when I gloried in the page
Of radiant singer and anointed sage.
Greece was my lamp: burnt out for lack of oil;
Rome, Python Rome, prey of its robber spoil!

All structures built upon a narrow space
Must fall, from having not your hosts for base.
O thrice must one be you, to see them shift
Along their desert flats, here dash, there drift;
With faith, that of privations and spilt blood,
Comes Reason armed to clear or bank the flood!
And thrice must one be you, to wait release
From duress in the swamp of their increase.
At which oppressive scene, beyond arrest,
A darkness not with stars of heaven dressed,
Philosophers behold; desponding view.
Your Many nourished, starved my brilliant few;
Then flinging heels, as charioteers the reins,
Dive down the fumy AEtna of their brains.
Belated vessels on a rising sea,
They seem: they pass!

- But not Philosophy!

- Ay, be we faithful to ourselves: despise
Nought but the coward in us! That way lies
The wisdom making passage through our slough.
Am I not heard, my head to Earth shall bow;
Like her, shall wait to see, and seeing wait.
Philosophy is Life's one match for Fate.
That photosphere of our high fountain One,
Our spirit's Lord and Reason's fostering sun,
Philosophy, shall light us in the shade,
Warm in the frost, make Good our aim and aid.
Companioned by the sweetest, ay renewed,
Unconquerable, whose aim for aid is Good!
Advantage to the Many: that we name
God's voice; have there the surety in our aim.

This thought unto my sister do I owe,
And irony and satire off me throw.
They crack a childish whip, drive puny herds,
Where numbers crave their sustenance in words.
Now let the perils thicken: clearer seen,
Your Chieftain Mind mounts over them serene.
Who never yet of scattered lamps was born
To speed a world, a marching world to warn,
But sunward from the vivid Many springs,
Counts conquest but a step, and through disaster sings.

Fragments of the Iliad in English Hexameter Verse

Poem: The Invective of Achilles

[Iliad, B. I. V. 149]

"Heigh me! brazen of front, thou glutton for plunder, how can one,
Servant here to thy mandates, heed thee among our Achaians,
Either the mission hie on or stoutly do fight with the foemen!
I, not hither I fared on account of the spear-armed Trojans,
Pledged to the combat; they unto me have in nowise a harm done;
Never have they, of a truth, come lifting my horses or oxen;
Never in deep-soiled Phthia, the nurser of heroes, my harvests

Ravaged, they; for between us is numbered full many a darksome
Mountain, ay, therewith too the stretch of the windy sea-waters.
O hugely shameless! thee did we follow to hearten thee, justice
Pluck from the Dardans for him, Menelaos, thee too, thou dog-eyed!
Whereof little thy thought is, nought whatever thou reckest.
Worse, it is thou whose threat 'tis to ravish my prize from me, portion
Won with much labour, the which my gift from the sons of Achaia.
Never, in sooth, have I known my prize equal thine when Achaians
Gave some flourishing populous Trojan town up to pillage.
Nay, sure, mine were the hands did most in the storm of the combat,
Yet when came peradventure share of the booty amongst us,
Bigger to thee went the prize, while I some small blessed thing bore
Off to the ships, my share of reward for my toil in the bloodshed!
So now go I to Phthia, for better by much it beseems me
Homeward go with my beaked ships now, and I hold not in prospect,
I being outraged, thou mayst gather here plunder and wealth-store."

Poem: The Invective of Achilles--V. 225

"Bibber besotted, with scowl of a cur, having heart of a deer, thou!
Never to join to thy warriors armed for the press of the conflict,
Never for ambush forth with the princeliest sons of Achaia
Dared thy soul, for to thee that thing would have looked as a death-stroke.
Sooth, more easy it seems, down the lengthened array of Achaians,
Snatch at the prize of the one whose voice has been lifted against thee.
Ravening king of the folk, for that thou hast thy rule over abjects;
Else, son of Atreus, now were this outrage on me thy last one.
Nay, but I tell thee, and I do swear a big oath on it likewise:
Yea, by the sceptre here, and it surely bears branches and leaf-buds

Never again, since first it was lopped from its trunk on the mountains,
No more sprouting; for round it all clean has the sharp metal clipped off
Leaves and the bark; ay, verify now do the sons of Achaia,
Guardian hands of the counsels of Zeus, pronouncing the judgement,
Hold it aloft; so now unto thee shall the oath have its portent;
Loud will the cry for Achilles burst from the sons of Achaia
Throughout the army, and thou chafe powerless, though in an anguish,
How to give succour when vast crops down under man-slaying Hector
Tumble expiring; and thou deep in thee shalt tear at thy heart-strings,
Rage-wrung, thou, that in nought thou didst honour the flower of Achaians."

Poem: Marshalling Of The Achaians

[Iliad, B. II V. 455]

Like as a terrible fire feeds fast on a forest enormous,
Up on a mountain height, and the blaze of it radiates round far,
So on the bright blest arms of the host in their march did the splendour
Gleam wide round through the circle of air right up to the sky-vault.
They, now, as when swarm thick in the air multitudinous winged flocks,
Be it of geese or of cranes or the long-necked troops of the wild-swans,
Off that Asian mead, by the flow of the waters of Kaistros;
Hither and yon fly they, and rejoicing in pride of their pinions,
Clamour, shaped to their ranks, and the mead all about them resoundeth;
So those numerous tribes from their ships and their shelterings poured forth
On that plain of Scamander, and horrible rumbled beneath them
Earth to the quick-paced feet of the men and the tramp of the horse-

hooves.
Stopped they then on the fair-flower'd field of Scamander, their thousands
Many as leaves and the blossoms born of the flowerful season.
Even as countless hot-pressed flies in their multitudes traverse,
Clouds of them, under some herdsman's wonning, where then are the milk-pails
Also, full of their milk, in the bountiful season of spring-time;
Even so thickly the long-haired sons of Achaia the plain held,
Prompt for the dash at the Trojan host, with the passion to crush them.
Those, likewise, as the goatherds, eyeing their vast flocks of goats, know
Easily one from the other when all get mixed o'er the pasture,
So did the chieftains rank them here there in their places for onslaught,
Hard on the push of the fray; and among them King Agamemnon,
He, for his eyes and his head, as when Zeus glows glad in his thunder,
He with the girdle of Ares, he with the breast of Poseidon.

Poem: Agamemnon In The Fight

[Iliad, B. XI. V. 148]

These, then, he left, and away where ranks were now clashing the thickest,
Onward rushed, and with him rushed all of the bright-greaved Achaians.
Foot then footmen slew, that were flying from direful compulsion,
Horse at the horsemen (up from off under them mounted the dust-cloud,
Up off the plain, raised up cloud-thick by the thundering horse-hooves)
Hewed with the sword's sharp edge; and so meanwhile Lord Agamemnon
Followed, chasing and slaughtering aye, on-urgeing the Argives.

Now, as when fire voracious catches the unclipped woodland,

This way bears it and that the great whirl of the wind, and the scrubwood
Stretches uptorn, flung forward alength by the fire's fury rageing,
So beneath Atreides Agamemnon heads of the scattered
Trojans fell; and in numbers amany the horses, neck-stiffened,
Rattled their vacant cars down the roadway gaps of the war-field,
Missing the blameless charioteers, but, for these, they were outstretched
Flat upon earth, far dearer to vultures than to their home-mates.

Poem: Paris And Diomedes

[Iliad; B. XI V. 378]

So he, with a clear shout of laughter,
Forth of his ambush leapt, and he vaunted him, uttering thiswise:
"Hit thou art! not in vain flew the shaft; how by rights it had pierced thee
Into the undermost gut, therewith to have rived thee of life-breath!
Following that had the Trojans plucked a new breath from their direst,
They all frighted of thee, as the goats bleat in flight from a lion."
Then unto him untroubled made answer stout Diomedes:
"Bow-puller, jiber, thy bow for thy glorying, spyer at virgins!
If that thou dared'st face me here out in the open with weapons,
Nothing then would avail thee thy bow and thy thick shot of arrows.
Now thou plumest thee vainly because of a graze of my footsole;
Reck I as were that stroke from a woman or some pettish infant.
Aye flies blunted the dart of the man that's emasculate, noughtworth!
Otherwise hits, forth flying from me, and but strikes it the slightest,
My keen shaft, and it numbers a man of the dead fallen straightway.
Torn, troth, then are the cheeks of the wife of that man fallen slaughtered,
Orphans his babes, full surely he reddens the earth with his blood-drops,

Rotting, round him the birds, more numerous they than the women."

Poem: Hypnos On Ida

[Iliad, B. XIV. V. 283]

They then to fountain-abundant Ida, mother of wild beasts,
Came, and they first left ocean to fare over mainland at Lektos,
Where underneath of their feet waved loftiest growths of the woodland.
There hung Hypnos fast, ere the vision of Zeus was observant,
Mounted upon a tall pine-tree, tallest of pines that on Ida
Lustily spring off soil for the shoot up aloft into aether.
There did he sit well-cloaked by the wide-branched pine for concealment,
That loud bird, in his form like, that perched high up in the mountains,
Chalkis is named by the Gods, but of mortals known as Kymindis.

Poem: Clash In Arms Of The Achaians And Trojans

[Iliad, B. XIV. V. 394]

Not the sea-wave so bellows abroad when it bursts upon shingle,
Whipped from the sea's deeps up by the terrible blast of the Northwind;
Nay, nor is ever the roar of the fierce fire's rush so arousing,
Down along mountain-glades, when it surges to kindle a woodland;

Nay, nor so tonant thunders the stress of the gale in the oak-trees'
Foliage-tresses high, when it rages to raveing its utmost;
As rose then stupendous the Trojan's cry and Achaians',
Dread upshouting as one when together they clashed in the conflict.

Poem: The Horses Of Achilles

[Iliad, B. XVII. V. 426]

So now the horses of Aiakides, off wide of the war-ground,
Wept, since first they were ware of their charioteer overthrown there,
Cast down low in the whirl of the dust under man-slaying Hector.
Sooth, meanwhile, then did Automedon, brave son of Diores,
Oft, on the one hand, urge them with flicks of the swift whip, and oft, too,
Coax entreatingly, hurriedly; whiles did he angrily threaten.
Vainly, for these would not to the ships, to the Hellespont spacious,
Backward turn, nor be whipped to the battle among the Achaians.
Nay, as a pillar remains immovable, fixed on the tombstone,
Haply, of some dead man or it may be a woman there-under;
Even like hard stood they there attached to the glorious war-car,
Earthward bowed with their heads; and of them so lamenting incessant
Ran the hot teardrops downward on to the earth from their eyelids,
Mourning their charioteer; all their lustrous manes dusty-clotted,
Right side and left of the yoke-ring tossed, to the breadth of the yoke-bow.
Now when the issue of Kronos beheld that sorrow, his head shook
Pitying them for their grief, these words then he spake in his bosom;
"Why, ye hapless, gave we to Peleus you, to a mortal
Master; ye that are ageless both, ye both of you deathless!
Was it that ye among men most wretched should come to have heart-grief?

'Tis most true, than the race of these men is there wretcheder nowhere
Aught over earth's range found that is gifted with breath and has movement."

Poem: The Mares Of The Camargue

[From the Mireio of Mistral]

A hundred mares, all white! their manes
Like mace-reed of the marshy plains
Thick-tufted, wavy, free o' the shears:
And when the fiery squadron rears
Bursting at speed, each mane appears
Even as the white scarf of a fay
Floating upon their necks along the heavens away.

O race of humankind, take shame!
For never yet a hand could tame,
Nor bitter spur that rips the flanks subdue
The mares of the Camargue. I have known,
By treason snared, some captives shown;
Expatriate from their native Rhone,
Led off, their saline pastures far from view:

And on a day, with prompt rebound,
They have flung their riders to the ground,
And at a single gallop, scouring free,
Wide-nostril'd to the wind, twice ten
Of long marsh-leagues devour'd, and then,

Back to the Vacares again,
After ten years of slavery just to breathe salt sea

For of this savage race unbent,
The ocean is the element.
Of old escaped from Neptune's car, full sure,
Still with the white foam fleck'd are they,
And when the sea puffs black from grey,
And ships part cables, loudly neigh
The stallions of Camargue, all joyful in the roar;

And keen as a whip they lash and crack
Their tails that drag the dust, and back
Scratch up the earth, and feel, entering their flesh, where he,
The God, drives deep his trident teeth,
Who in one horror, above, beneath,
Bids storm and watery deluge seethe,
And shatters to their depths the abysses of the sea.

Cant. iv.

www.bookjungle.com email: sales@bookjungle.com fax: 630-214-0564 mail: Book Jungle PO Box 2226 Champaign, IL 61825

The Codes Of Hammurabi And Moses
W. W. Davies

The discovery of the Hammurabi Code is one of the greatest achievements of archaeology, and is of paramount interest, not only to the student of the Bible, but also to all those interested in ancient history...

Religion **ISBN:** *1-59462-338-4* **Pages:** 132 *MSRP $12.95* QTY

The Theory of Moral Sentiments
Adam Smith

This work from 1749. contains original theories of conscience amd moral judgment and it is the foundation for systemof morals.

Philosophy **ISBN:** *1-59462-777-0* **Pages:** 536 *MSRP $19.95* QTY

Jessica's First Prayer
Hesba Stretton

In a screened and secluded corner of one of the many railway-bridges which span the streets of London there could be seen a few years ago, from five o'clock every morning until half past eight, a tidily set-out coffee-stall, consisting of a trestle and board, upon which stood two large tin cans, with a small fire of charcoal burning under each so as to keep the coffee boiling during the early hours of the morning when the work-people were thronging into the city on their way to their daily toil...

Childrens **ISBN:** *1-59462-373-2* **Pages:** 84 *MSRP $9.95* QTY

My Life and Work
Henry Ford

Henry Ford revolutionized the world with his implementation of mass production for the Model T automobile. Gain valuable business insight into his life and work with his own auto-biography... "We have only started on our development of our country we have not as yet, with all our talk of wonderful progress, done more than scratch the surface. The progress has been wonderful enough but..."

Biographies/ **ISBN:** *1-59462-198-5* **Pages:** 300 *MSRP $21.95* QTY

www.bookjungle.com *email: sales@bookjungle.com fax: 630-214-0564 mail: Book Jungle PO Box 2226 Champaign, IL 61825*

The Art of Cross-Examination
Francis Wellman

QTY

I presume it is the experience of every author, after his first book is published upon an important subject, to be almost overwhelmed with a wealth of ideas and illustrations which could readily have been included in his book, and which to his own mind, at least, seem to make a second edition inevitable. Such certainly was the case with me; and when the first edition had reached its sixth impression in five months, I rejoiced to learn that it seemed to my publishers that the book had met with a sufficiently favorable reception to justify a second and considerably enlarged edition. ..

Reference   ISBN: *1-59462-647-2*   Pages:412   MSRP *$19.95*

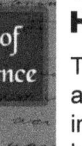

On the Duty of Civil Disobedience
Henry David Thoreau

QTY

Thoreau wrote his famous essay, On the Duty of Civil Disobedience, as a protest against an unjust but popular war and the immoral but popular institution of slave-owning. He did more than write—he declined to pay his taxes, and was hauled off to gaol in consequence. Who can say how much this refusal of his hastened the end of the war and of slavery ?

Law   ISBN: *1-59462-747-9*   Pages:48   MSRP *$7.45*

Dream Psychology Psychoanalysis for Beginners
Sigmund Freud

QTY

Sigmund Freud, born Sigismund Schlomo Freud (May 6, 1856 - September 23, 1939), was a Jewish-Austrian neurologist and psychiatrist who co-founded the psychoanalytic school of psychology. Freud is best known for his theories of the unconscious mind, especially involving the mechanism of repression; his redefinition of sexual desire as mobile and directed towards a wide variety of objects; and his therapeutic techniques, especially his understanding of transference in the therapeutic relationship and the presumed value of dreams as sources of insight into unconscious desires.

Psychology   ISBN: *1-59462-905-6*   Pages:196   MSRP *$15.45*

The Miracle of Right Thought
Orison Swett Marden

QTY

Believe with all of your heart that you will do what you were made to do. When the mind has once formed the habit of holding cheerful, happy, prosperous pictures, it will not be easy to form the opposite habit. It does not matter how improbable or how far away this realization may see, or how dark the prospects may be, if we visualize them as best we can, as vividly as possible, hold tenaciously to them and vigorously struggle to attain them, they will gradually become actualized, realized in the life. But a desire, a longing without endeavor, a yearning abandoned or held indifferently will vanish without realization.

Self Help   ISBN: *1-59462-644-8*   Pages:360   MSRP *$25.45*

www.bookjungle.com email: sales@bookjungle.com fax: 630-214-0564 mail: Book Jungle PO Box 2226 Champaign, IL 61825

QTY

	Title	ISBN	Price
☐	**The Rosicrucian Cosmo-Conception Mystic Christianity** by *Max Heindel*	ISBN: *1-59462-188-8*	$38.95

The Rosicrucian Cosmo-conception is not dogmatic, neither does it appeal to any other authority than the reason of the student. It is: not controversial, but is: sent forth in the, hope that it may help to clear...
New Age/Religion Pages 646

☐ **Abandonment To Divine Providence** by *Jean-Pierre de Caussade* ISBN: *1-59462-228-0* $25.95
"The Rev. Jean Pierre de Caussade was one of the most remarkable spiritual writers of the Society of Jesus in France in the 18th Century. His death took place at Toulouse in 1751. His works have gone through many editions and have been republished...
Inspirational/Religion Pages 400

☐ **Mental Chemistry** by *Charles Haanel* ISBN: *1-59462-192-6* $23.95
Mental Chemistry allows the change of material conditions by combining and appropriately utilizing the power of the mind. Much like applied chemistry creates something new and unique out of careful combinations of chemicals the mastery of mental chemistry...
New Age Pages 354

☐ **The Letters of Robert Browning and Elizabeth Barret Barrett 1845-1846 vol II** ISBN: *1-59462-193-4* $35.95
by *Robert Browning* and *Elizabeth Barrett*
Biographies Pages 596

☐ **Gleanings In Genesis (volume I)** by *Arthur W. Pink* ISBN: *1-59462-130-6* $27.45
Appropriately has Genesis been termed "the seed plot of the Bible" for in it we have, in germ form, almost all of the great doctrines which are afterwards fully developed in the books of Scripture which follow...
Religion/Inspirational Pages 420

☐ **The Master Key** by *L. W. de Laurence* ISBN: *1-59462-001-6* $30.95
In no branch of human knowledge has there been a more lively increase of the spirit of research during the past few years than in the study of Psychology, Concentration and Mental Discipline. The requests for authentic lessons in Thought Control, Mental Discipline and... New Age/Business Pages 422

☐ **The Lesser Key Of Solomon Goetia** by *L. W. de Laurence* ISBN: *1-59462-092-X* $9.95
This translation of the first book of the "Lernegton" which is now for the first time made accessible to students of Talismanic Magic was done, after careful collation and edition, from numerous Ancient Manuscripts in Hebrew, Latin, and French...
New Age/Occult Pages 92

☐ **Rubaiyat Of Omar Khayyam** by *Edward Fitzgerald* ISBN:*1-59462-332-5* $13.95
Edward Fitzgerald, whom the world has already learned, in spite of his own efforts to remain within the shadow of anonymity, to look upon as one of the rarest poets of the century, was born at Bredfield, in Suffolk, on the 31st of March, 1809. He was the third son of John Purcell...
Music Pages 172

☐ **Ancient Law** by *Henry Maine* ISBN: *1-59462-128-4* $29.95
The chief object of the following pages is to indicate some of the earliest ideas of mankind, as they are reflected in Ancient Law, and to point out the relation of those ideas to modern thought.
Religion/History Pages 452

☐ **Far-Away Stories** by *William J. Locke* ISBN: *1-59462-129-2* $19.45
"Good wine needs no bush, but a collection of mixed vintages does. And this book is just such a collection. Some of the stories I do not want to remain buried for ever in the museum files of dead magazine-numbers an author's not unpardonable vanity..."
Fiction Pages 272

☐ **Life of David Crockett** by *David Crockett* ISBN: *1-59462-250-7* $27.45
"Colonel David Crockett was one of the most remarkable men of the times in which he lived. Born in humble life, but gifted with a strong will, an indomitable courage, and unremitting perseverance...
Biographies/New Age Pages 424

☐ **Lip-Reading** by *Edward Nitchie* ISBN: *1-59462-206-X* $25.95
Edward B. Nitchie, founder of the New York School for the Hard of Hearing, now the Nitchie School of Lip-Reading, Inc, wrote "LIP-READING Principles and Practice". The development and perfecting of this meritorious work on lip-reading was an undertaking...
How-to Pages 400

☐ **A Handbook of Suggestive Therapeutics, Applied Hypnotism, Psychic Science** ISBN: *1-59462-214-0* $24.95
by *Henry Munro*
Health/New Age/Health/Self-help Pages 376

☐ **A Doll's House: and Two Other Plays** by *Henrik Ibsen* ISBN: *1-59462-112-8* $19.95
Henrik Ibsen created this classic when in revolutionary 1848 Rome. Introducing some striking concepts in playwriting for the realist genre, this play has been studied the world over.
Fiction/Classics/Plays 308

☐ **The Light of Asia** by *sir Edwin Arnold* ISBN: *1-59462-204-3* $13.95
In this poetic masterpiece, Edwin Arnold describes the life and teachings of Buddha. The man who was to become known as Buddha to the world was born as Prince Gautama of India but he rejected the worldly riches and abandoned the reigns of power when... Religion/History/Biographies Pages 170

☐ **The Complete Works of Guy de Maupassant** by *Guy de Maupassant* ISBN: *1-59462-157-8* $16.95
"For days and days, nights and nights, I had dreamed of that first kiss which was to consecrate our engagement, and I knew not on what spot I should put my lips..."
Fiction/Classics Pages 240

☐ **The Art of Cross-Examination** by *Francis L. Wellman* ISBN: *1-59462-309-0* $26.95
Written by a renowned trial lawyer, Wellman imparts his experience and uses case studies to explain how to use psychology to extract desired information through questioning.
How-to/Science/Reference Pages 408

☐ **Answered or Unanswered?** by *Louisa Vaughan* ISBN: *1-59462-248-5* $10.95
Miracles of Faith in China
Religion Pages 112

☐ **The Edinburgh Lectures on Mental Science (1909)** by *Thomas* ISBN: *1-59462-008-3* $11.95
This book contains the substance of a course of lectures recently given by the writer in the Queen Street Hall, Edinburgh. Its purpose is to indicate the Natural Principles governing the relation between Mental Action and Material Conditions...
New Age/Psychology Pages 148

☐ **Ayesha** by *H. Rider Haggard* ISBN: *1-59462-301-5* $24.95
Verily and indeed it is the unexpected that happens! Probably if there was one person upon the earth from whom the Editor of this, and of a certain previous history, did not expect to hear again...
Classics Pages 380

☐ **Ayala's Angel** by *Anthony Trollope* ISBN: *1-59462-352-X* $29.95
The two girls were both pretty, but Lucy who was twenty-one who supposed to be simple and comparatively unattractive, whereas Ayala was credited, as her Bombwhat romantic name might show, with poetic charm and a taste for romance. Ayala when her father died was nineteen...
Fiction Pages 484

☐ **The American Commonwealth** by *James Bryce* ISBN: *1-59462-286-8* $34.45
An interpretation of American democratic political theory. It examines political mechanics and society from the perspective of Scotsman James Bryce
Politics Pages 572

☐ **Stories of the Pilgrims** by *Margaret P. Pumphrey* ISBN: *1-59462-116-0* $17.95
This book explores pilgrims religious oppression in England as well as their escape to Holland and eventual crossing to America on the Mayflower, and their early days in New England...
History Pages 268

www.bookjungle.com email: sales@bookjungle.com fax: 630-214-0564 mail: Book Jungle PO Box 2226 Champaign, IL 61825

QTY

The Fasting Cure by *Sinclair Upton* ISBN: *1-59462-222-1* **$13.95**
In the Cosmopolitan Magazine for May, 1910, and in the Contemporary Review (London) for April, 1910, I published an article dealing with my experiences in fasting. I have written a great many magazine articles, but never one which attracted so much attention... New Age/Self Help/Health Pages 164

Hebrew Astrology by *Sepharial* ISBN: *1-59462-308-2* **$13.45**
In these days of advanced thinking it is a matter of common observation that we have left many of the old landmarks behind and that we are now pressing forward to greater heights and to a wider horizon than that which represented the mind-content of our progenitors... Astrology Pages 144

Thought Vibration or The Law of Attraction in the Thought World ISBN: *1-59462-127-6* **$12.95**
by *William Walker Atkinson* Psychology/Religion Pages 144

Optimism by *Helen Keller* ISBN: *1-59462-108-X* **$15.95**
Helen Keller was blind, deaf, and mute since 19 months old, yet famously learned how to overcome these handicaps, communicate with the world, and spread her lectures promoting optimism. An inspiring read for everyone... Biographies/Inspirational Pages 84

Sara Crewe by *Frances Burnett* ISBN: *1-59462-360-0* **$9.45**
In the first place, Miss Minchin lived in London. Her home was a large, dull, tall one, in a large, dull square, where all the houses were alike, and all the sparrows were alike, and where all the door-knockers made the same heavy sound... Childrens/Classic Pages 88

The Autobiography of Benjamin Franklin by *Benjamin Franklin* ISBN: *1-59462-135-7* **$24.95**
The Autobiography of Benjamin Franklin has probably been more extensively read than any other American historical work, and no other book of its kind has had such ups and downs of fortune. Franklin lived for many years in England, where he was agent... Biographies/History Pages 332

Name	
Email	
Telephone	
Address	
City, State ZIP	

☐ Credit Card   ☐ Check / Money Order

Credit Card Number	
Expiration Date	
Signature	

Please Mail to: Book Jungle
                  PO Box 2226
                  Champaign, IL 61825
or Fax to: 630-214-0564

ORDERING INFORMATION

web: *www.bookjungle.com*
email: *sales@bookjungle.com*
fax: *630-214-0564*
mail: *Book Jungle PO Box 2226 Champaign, IL 61825*
or PayPal *to sales@bookjungle.com*

Please contact us for bulk discounts

DIRECT-ORDER TERMS

**20% Discount if You Order
Two or More Books**
Free Domestic Shipping!
Accepted: Master Card, Visa,
Discover, American Express

www.ingramcontent.com/pod-product-compliance
Lightning Source LLC
Chambersburg PA
CBHW081327040426
42453CB00013B/2323